CW00811904

For the BPs —
my own harvest home

First published in Great Britain by Parvenu Press 2018

Copyright of poems remains with the author

Cover Design: Vicky Sharman
Typeset by: dit@ntlworld.com

Printed by: imprintdigital.com
Seychelles Farm, Upton Pyne, UK
EX5 5HY

This book is sold subject to the condition that it shall not, by way of trade or otherwise, be lent, resold, hired out, or otherwise circulated without the publisher's prior consent in any form of binding or cover other than that in which it is published.

ISBN: 978-0-9929490-3-7

Parvenu Press: parvenupress@gmail.com

Cover illustration: *The Harvesters* (artist unknown)

Those Under Saturn

Selected Poems

Stephen Plaice

To Kathy
with all my love
Steve
March '25

P

PARVENU
PRESS

Acknowledgements

Some of the poems in this volumes previously appeared in *The London Magazine, PEN Anthology 1, The Forward Book of Poetry 1994, The Cumberland Review, The Honest Ulsterman, Orbis* and *Poetry Nottingham.*

A Lifer in Summer was first broadcast on BBC Radio 4 as part of *Soundtrack,* an account of the author's residency at HMP Lewes. Together with *Giants* it was published in *The Fonthill Poets,* Parvenu Press 2016. *Harvest Home* first appeared in *Poetry South East 2000.*

The title poem *Those Under Saturn* first appeared as part of the libretto of *The Io Passion* (music by Harrison Birtwistle) in 2004. The copyright is with Boosey and Hawkes Ltd. *Eight Gates to the Rain in the Streets* first appeared as part of the libretto of *The Finnish Prisoner* in 2007 (music by Orlando Gough).

Poetry by the same author

Poems (with Martyn Ford) Parvenu Press 1982
Rumours of Cousins Yorick Books 1983
Over The Rollers Yorick Books 1992
The Fonthill Poets (edited with Martyn Ford)
Parvenu Press 2016

Foreword

These selected poems are a combination of my published and unpublished work from 1979 until 2018. They are presented almost chronologically in six sections. The early sections roughly coincide with my published volumes up to 1994. I was a member of the Fonthill Poets who were active in the South East from the late Seventies until the mid Nineties, and many of these poems were read at Fonthill meetings.

The third section of the book represents a selection of the verse I wrote during my seven-year prison residency at Lewes Prison in Sussex between 1987 and 1994, a selection of which I have collected here under the title *Eight Gates to the Rain in the Streets*. I supply a glossary to these poems at the end of that section.

A selection of my later verse appears here under the title *Tending the Hop*. I also include a section of muse poems, *Eden II*, which somehow found their own order. Finally, I append *Harvest Home*, mostly recent pieces that seem conclusive.

My thanks to fellow Fonthill member Martyn Ford for editing this collection, and to Vicky Sharman and John Bridger for their care in its production.

And all was for an apple
An apple that he took…

Adam lay ybounden
15th century

Contents

1. Rumours of Cousins

The Sleeping Village 10
The Man Who Steals Behind Me 12
To the Young Dead 1914-18 14
Methods of Protection 16
Through the French Windows 17
Rumours of Cousins 19
The Cluster Theory at Beachy Head 21
Tea With the Divorcees 22
Non Sancta Sum Omnibus 24
Lisette 26

2. Over the Rollers

Over the Rollers 28
In Dockland 29
Photosynthesis 30
The Ghosts of the Victorians 31
The Brewery 33
The Last Barge 34
First Bus 35
On Leaving a Provincial Town 36
Last Cafe in the West 37
Renaissance Steps 38
The Bull Among the Poppies 39
The Roman Returns 41
The Man to Trust 43
Fallow 44
The Landscape 46

3. Eight Gates to the Rain in the Streets

Giants 48
The Photographer's Chair 50
Midday Bang-up 51
A Lifer in Summer 52
Invitation to a Cell 53
End of Shift 54
Bonfire Night 55
Visiting Wives 56
Forget-Me-Not 57
Jackdaws 58
The Prison Cricket 59
Child of the Prison 60
Maundy Thursday on the Exercise Yard 61
The Shadow Board 62
On the Doors of B Wing 64

A Laugh in the Hospital 66
Spends 67
A Quiet Day in the County Gaol 68
Suspendatur 70
The Copper Beech 71
The Last Man Out 72
Eight Gates to the Rain in the Streets 73
Glossary of Prison Terms 74

4. *Tending the Hop*
Siren 78
Grünewald's Madonna 80
The Hop Exchange 81
Tending the Hop 82
In the Flax Field 84
Those Under Saturn 85
One Street Back 86
Serpentine 88
The Acid Bottles 89
Manifest Destiny 90
At Licton Springs 91
The Sun Machine 92
Urban Fox 94

5. *Eden II*
Midsummer Moon 96
Just Before 97
A Return to Mithymna 98
The Spark 99
In Verona Perhaps 100
Stained Glass 101
The Notebook 102
At the Florist's 103
Lovelight 104
The Corner Table 105
The Harbour 106
Sussex Blues 107
Eden II 108

6. *Harvest Home*
Canal Time 110
Gabriel 112
Helen 115
Chichester Walls 116
Brighton Wall 118
The Sycamore Declines 119
On Falmer Pond 120
Harvest Home 122

1. Rumours of Cousins

The Sleeping Village

If we walked long enough in this heat,
our ears attuned to the half-heard hum,
following a spire and a weather-vane,
we might again enter that contented street,
the one down which no coaches come,
drink in the wafting ale-house reek,
and watch the men through mullioned windows
lobbing their toads in the leaden hole.*

If we walked long enough in this heat,
we might hear the afternoon broadly speak
the broken dialect of these Downs,
the smith clamping nails in his rotten teeth,
the treddle beneath the potter's feet,
the widow spinning her yards of sleep.

If we walked long enough in this heat,
we might take the elm-shaded seat,
relive the centuries scored on the green,
and imagine the poets we might have been
approving the scene from the boundary.

The sweet hay stored in the dormant barn,
the delirious flies on the rich muck-heap,
if we walked long enough in this heat,
what half-fledged memories we might meet,
faces seen on roads forgotten,
landscapes put away like postcards,
the books we never did complete,
the partners who drifted back into the market-place.

In the churchyard we might even greet
all our incidental dead arisen,
those the wasted years imprison,
casting off their winding-sheet
to walk with us down the evening lane
till the last bird answers the last sheep's bleat.

Could we ignore the signposts, trust our feet,
attune our ears to the half-heard hum,
follow a spire and a weather-vane,
we might again enter that contented street
and awaken the sleeping village,
if we went deeper into these hills,
if we walked long enough in this heat.

*toads — an old Sussex pub game, toad-in-the-hole. A heavy coin, a
'toad', is thrown from a distance into a hole in a lead-covered box.

The Man Who Steals Behind Me

When turning back on certain roads,
I have seen the conspiring trees conceal
the man who steals behind me,
all that I have known he knows,
all that I have felt he feels.
Along the paths my feet have trodden
he whistles the tunes I have forgotten,
rambles through my neglected days,
blown by the aimless winds
that play down unadopted lanes
and sweep the cold, deserted fields.

When turning back in certain towns,
I have seen a closing door conceal
the man who steals behind me,
all that I have thought he thinks,
all that I have coined he steals.
In bars where former friends still drink,
he refills the glass I drained,
spouts the stale ideas once framed
in the bright and bevelled mirrors
where my spitting image revelled
with my forsaken companies.

When turning back on certain rooms,
I have seen a shifting eye conceal
the man who steals behind me,
all those that I have loved he loves,
all those that I have hurt he heals.
In last night's hotel he entertains
women in whose arms I have lain,
repeats my plausible appeals
to pretty felicity to marry me
and live as plain fidelity.
He sleeps with my missed eternities.

When turning back on certain roads,
I have seen the growing dark conceal
the man who steals behind me.
He is the space that I have filled,
all that I become, he is still to be.
Once I thought he followed,
but the longer that I walk I feel
that man steals away from me,
and there beyond the furthest tree
it is not a death that stalks behind,
but a life departing from my heels.

To the Young Dead 1914-18

Sleep deeper now history has the set,
the last of all your comrades dead,
having lived the broader stretch and seen
the bee collect fifty summers in his sack.
And in those sprawling years having known
a woman's body age beside their own,
children's voices sing high and crack,
the extended quiet of the house
that little in old age disturbs,
even in the senile chair's deep recess
understood perhaps the migration of the birds,
and felt, unlike you, a gradual decline
blending into the landscape of their lives.

While you in uniform with stony stares
have witnessed from cold public plinths
the wild fling of our great affairs,
heard us on each other's doorsteps peddle
the romantic software of our minds,
and meddle with our little feelings,
pretending for them grand designs.
You have thought no doubt of sacrifice,
the great word that sustained you in the mud,
and of all those decent girls in your pockets
who married others when the grief had ebbed,
you have thought perhaps and reconsidered
since what you died for now itself is dead.

Still we approve your doomed platoon
trooping into the trenches of conviction,
for that authentic act remains,
even if the words for which your lives
were wasted have grown meaningless.

Your youth forever framed in death
stiffens us a moment at the mantelpiece
and makes us wonder if we could forsake
all the warm refuges that are open to us
and storm forward to the ideal sacrifice.
But you too, watching us, you must regret
that you did not hesitate, grow old and love
imperfectly as we have done.

Methods of Protection

More insistent now the squabbling of the gulls,
the neighbour's children's plaintive games,
as we wake with hangovers under high ceilings
in the warm embrace of unfamiliar flesh.
Shall we begin the candid talk afresh,
or silently respect the limits to our truths?
You I have known, but in the darkness —
we have coupled and uncoupled
at a remote junction of the night,
shared the body's moment of distress,
when all but this was meaningless —
there was a bottle, there was a bed,
perhaps that is all that should be said.

Now there are methods of protection,
and we need not hesitate to give ourselves
to the sensations of a stranger,
or to drift into an infinity of others,
making of passing friends our lovers,
knowing that they present no danger,
no menace to the lives that we project.
Yet something, certainly, is disappointed,
— it is there at the breakfast table —
some dull twinge of ancestry perhaps,
waking the spirit of that mutual belonging
that we for these few seaside years yet,
by youth protected, may still neglect.

Through the French Windows

A little money has come to us at last
— our parents wished to see us settled—
and now we sit long into the afternoon
in the living-rooms we have decorated
with the trophies of our hectic travels,
immersed in our own fantastic music,
embroidering on the legends
of a wild youth barely tamed.

Sure now beyond our first romantic flushes,
we lounge content among our wives
whose beauty was the shortlived craze
that lured us into this half-kept promise.
Their faces are softer now, more comfortable
for having lost the sharp daemon that once beset us,
our jealous passions appeased by time,
our passing time by love.

Over tea we set aside the cup to emphasize
Some special wisdom gleaned from our professions
— we had never suspected there was so much
to the careers to which our parents pressed us —
really very fascinating when you get to know
the subtle ways that money moves.
Is that really the feckless schoolboy speaking
who once, with us, trapped sticklebacks?

Outside the summer turns in its sleep,
animating the leaves, dappling the carpet.
Our talk subsides, and a few gardens away
the children's voices mingle again in the heat.
There is the smell of cooking from the kitchen,
someone singing snatches of the latest hit;
the couples join hands and silently defect
to investigate the glorious borders.

While through the French windows
the old Green Man with bow-string slack
peers in at the conference of empty chairs
and the plundered tea-tray, reviews
the cooling debris of our reality,
before seeking once more the camouflage of the shrubbery,
unseen host to our incidental music
in the permanent summer of his garden.

Rumours of Cousins

At thirty we long to begin again,
to bring order to our bookshelves
and tinker with our dormant convictions,
but instead the children come crying
into the silence where we once read,
demanding where we ourselves demanded,
and our lives spread out like magazines
with regular features but no great themes.
Eventually, living follows thought no longer,
but thought living, and stronger links
chain our thoughts to the everyday.
We find ourselves absorbed in manuals,
descriptions of the hardy annuals,
or the many reasons recipes fail.
We make our daily diet substantial,
take pleasure in the meals and bedtimes,
in waking with the same arms round us,
for we may now afford ourselves some comfort
and approve at last our own familiar reality
condensing around the kitchen table.

To be the author of all this flesh
has brought a certain happiness,
but sometimes weeding in a border,
or sorting in a confused cupboard,
sometimes at dusk drawing the curtains,
there come rumours of cousins,
possible existences long since terminated,
versed in spectacular philosophies,
polyglottal from continuous travel,
wearing the smile of another knowledge,
mysteries we may not now unravel.

Another moment and we would welcome them,
like a constellation on a clear night,
but the crying comes, the louder mortal crying,
and we begin again to fuss and mother,
pretending this is our one firm life,
denying rumours of the unlived others.

The Cluster Theory at Beachy Head

*In fact Beachy Head has now developed such a reputation as a death spot that the **Eastbourne Medical Gazette** has published a three-page feature on it. This points to the curious incidence of 'clustering', when more than one person goes over the Head in a short space of time.*

I did not jump, I found the gap,
the soft tear in my own horizon,
left my licence and a family snap,
drained the bottle to the last drop,
no one restrained me or shouted stop,
not even the jackdaws made a flap.
The bare wish in the end was simply to be
no longer defined by the nagging wind.

That same day, from out at sea,
I saw him follow, then her the next.
The jackdaws held their own inquest,
but by now the coroner must have guessed,
there is a pattern to our final steps,
certain instinctive paths to the descent,
like the lanes down which the lemmings race,
and once one of us has found the place
where the nagging wind is weakest,
it makes it easier for the rest.

Now I watch you at the edge,
simulate the plunge with inner dread,
your sanity, my madness separated
by a single, soundless tread.
But you turn round, walk slowly back,
disturb the jackdaws in your tracks,
make wearily for the telephone box.
Could it be you did not find the gap?
It closes after several days perhaps.

Tea With the Divorcees

The weather has changed again in the windows,
and outside the garden now reflects
the growing disappointment of the early winter.
They have been talking all afternoon
in that sincere and convalescent tone
they have lately cultivated together,
for now, having known the limits of one love,
they are returned like stretched pullovers
to the unfamiliar contours of their own lives.

You sit sipping tea, refusing cigarettes,
Defer to more authentic disenchantment,
listening to their wounded lives recounted,
as a soldier who has seen no action yet.
You supply perhaps the odd vignette
of mutual acquaintances recently met
whose knots have slipped or minds have bent,
while watching Maria, her small devotions,
colonising the garden with her dolls.

Not one couple I know is happy —
she puts our memories to the test
  — our friends are the people we love best.
Yet you remember once their happiness
glided past you like a royal barge
bound for a picnic in lush meadows,
and they were sure of their bedfellows
and that their children would be blessed.
We have all lived in such deception.

The tea is fresh again in the pot,
and in the leaded windows you plot
Maria searching through the dusk.
And you? she asks, *Have you never thought...?*
We coelacanths are seldom caught!

They laugh, steady their uncertain cups,
You've always had a way with words.
Maria scolds the doll she had lost
among the wreckage of the irises.
No, words have had their way with me.

Non Sancta Sum Omnibus

(A possible reading of one fragment of the medieval graffiti to be seen in Ashwell Church, North Hertfordshire, which is the location for the poem.)

Those were the blackest years
and we deserved them,
plague, storm, the blossoming trees
turned upwards by their tails.
Our death was but a blink
of the all-seeing eye.
We were different men then,
enchanted by our own numeracy
and by the merest coincidence
of words and clouds and rhymes.
Those few of us who survived
scratched upon these pillars
the vestiges of our unshaken faith
in wretched dog-Latin,
hoping to appease Our Master.
But in daily dread we expected
the tower to be uprooted
by the roaring wrath we worshipped,
for we had known pleasure
in other's bodies, in our own minds,
enjoyed our good neighbour's misfortune
and coveted their big-breasted wives.
Those were the blackest years
and we deserved them,
for we were not holy at all.

Outside it is perfect April,
birds, bells, the blossoming trees
floating gently in the breeze.
In a recommended garden
we order trout and avocados,
ignoring the tower and the chimes.

We are different men now,
we nearly all survive,
taking our language for granted,
and most things in our stride,
the changing of seasons, landscapes, menus,
divorce, alimony, our second wives.
And should we fancy the girl on the next table,
imagine the silk purse she keeps between her thighs,
no pestilence will afflict the glands,
no storm of wrath will rack the land,
we have no vengeful God to fear.
These are our prosperous years
and we deserve them,
for we are not holy at all.

Lisette

We never actually met Lisette,
though everyone was talking about her,
her youth, her talents, her looks,
that she was the daughter
of the cellist and the flautist
of the London Symphony Orchestra.
Everyone was sorting out divorces
and squabbling over the children,
but they still found time
to talk about Lisette.
She came by one afternoon
when we were out walking,
she must have seen the mess
of our lives spread out across the table.
A couple of cups had been disturbed,
and a new flower was twisted in a vase.
The chairs were somehow emptier
than when we had left.
We knew it must have been Lisette,
her perfume was in the air,
and even though we do not expect her
to call this way again,
when we go out walking together,
we always leave the door open.

2. Over the Rollers

Over the Rollers

There are parties on the lower river tonight,
the winking lights of houseboats under the willows,
the soft glow of cabin-cruisers permanently arrived.
Music and laughter caress the waterline,
someone is shouting 'Surprise!' but it is more like
something we have all known for a very long time.
Among the mature purples the moon stands aside,
the hostess turns as if to welcome us on board,
but there is no smile, just a leer of disgust
as she casts her olive-stone accurately into the dark.

We are not going to that party,
nor to the others that flare along the banks.
There is something in us that wants to feel
the sudden snatch of cruel fingers above,
the tug of the sunken devil in the mud.
Up around Deadman's Bend, they say,
the pole slips into delicious nothingness,
and the water tastes of champagne as you drown.
We will own the places where we make love,
moaning there like fallen soldiers,
thirsting as the night wheels on.

In the morning, the crunch of clean gravel,
the lucid Sunday bells tumbling in the sky,
breakfast in the watermeadows upstream.
We will keep this dream of morning,
it will survive wherever I hurt you,
even when you are far away and buried
in the business of other people's lives.
It will come to you especially at night,
and uninvited to my endless river-parties,
with the moon and the young whispering:
Tonight, tonight,
Tonight we are going over the rollers.

In Dockland

Where the ships came in, dream me alive.
I wore a veil of estuary fog
and a hempen rope of hair.
A whistle could blow the veil aside,
a pull on the rope raise my skirts,
let the negroes and the lascars inside.
They gave me their tongues and their oils.
They were my cocoa and my tea.
One night the fog was ether,
it felt as if I took the crew on board.
You were my only child. You cost me.
I pushed you out into the world
cradled in an orange-crate — your first ship.
You were molasses, sweet child.
Did they refine you in the big house
and try to make you white?

I've looked for you often since,
along the wharves where the fog
used to curl around the woodpile.
It is permanently Sunday there,
all the captains have gone inland
to find a new religion.
They have invented the overhead lines.
As long as we go on I don't mind.
Your children are my children,
bring them to visit me sometimes,
and do not think badly when you sense
my delirious ghost soliciting
the gaunt warehouses now.
Don't dream the purity that was.
Whistle. Dream me alive.
You are the blend that I began.

Photosynthesis

When photography began, the world stopped.
The pony and trap held patiently still.
The farmer's wife in the doorway turned to stone.
The labourer with shouldered pitchfork
stiffened into his respectful pose ten paces
from the awkward earl enacting his daily stroll.
Only the unruly tree continued to swirl,
filtering the pale summer sunlight,
spoiling the edge of the treated plates.

When our ancestors began to picture themselves,
they wished to preserve their stationary world,
even though this is the very moment
from which we have measured its decline.
The labourers went quietly into the factories,
land values rose, the farm was sold, resold,
the track became a lane, the lane a road
which still bore the farmer's family name,
but a hundred families came to call home.

Slowly the pictures too began to move
and to occupy us for whole hours of the day.
Now we sit and watch a moving world,
see more than we could imagine alone
or ever experience for ourselves.
We observe the acts of love and death so often
— even follow the salmon journey of the sperm
and the transmigration of our astral souls —
they no longer move us to pleasure or to tears.

But sometimes when the images pall
and we step out, no further than the gate,
for a breath of the half-refreshing air,
stand motionless among the cars,
surveying the life of our suburban road,
it feels like we too are being observed
by something much more ingenious —
and there is the tree still absorbing light,
the oldest camera in the world.

The Ghosts of the Victorians

For her they were all in the future.
Who is that gentleman in the morning room
tinkering with the tip-tap machine?
Elly often frowned over one eye
and said things like this unnaturally
when they were quiet upstairs
and I had time for my needles.
Isn't that the tube Elly? I said and she went.
But then it quickened —
Nineteen-eighty-five-six, who'll live here then?
The Nabob of Krishnapur and his seven wives,
the Admiral of Her Majesty's balloons,
the inventor of the speaking lines…
It won't be no Davenports for sure,
their breath is as short as a thimble.
Elly I said *that's no way to talk in service.*
She was church-quiet, but then the frown came again.
Who is that lady in the morning room
Squinting at the click-clack machine?
Mrs Fanshawe — I whispered in the pantry,
that girl will be in Cold Harbour
before the sloes are ripe.
But it was the Fever took her.
The Doctor closed the frowning eye,
wiped his hands and said —
From that incestuous clan
of monkeys out at Storrington.
Too many dark nights and daughters.
He was a clever man the Doctor,
his linctus took away my cough,
but did nothing for Elly or Davenports alike.

I saw her once afterwards,
the day the youngest Master died,
she still had that frown over one eye —
Elly I said *does it hurt you still?*

She pointed upstairs. The tube whistled.
I went. He was dead. She was right.
Since then the charabanc, the aeroplane,
telephone, electric light,
Mrs Fanshawe could no longer manage the stairs.
Now the mistress is dead. The Doctor is dead.
Old Mr Davenport has a bell beside his bed.
The tube whistles sometimes in the middle of the night.
The children, bless them, still love a game.
For me they are all in the past.
I remember over my needles how Elly once said —
Nobody really lives here any more,
We are already safe, at home, on the farm.
I like to think of us there, all of us,
not here any more, not in this house
I will be the last to forget.

The Brewery

At primary school because I had *brains*
Mr Savage sat me by the sash-window
that looked out on the brewery.

Its walls fumed sweetly all morning,
black engines muscled in to catch
the barrels wobbling down the ramps.

The midday siren always beat the bell,
brought the workers out into the goalmouths
to take the chances missed in the match.

Summers came, the wasps; the chimney's shadow
grew long, seemed to pace the afternoon,
hold off the moment of escape. I ran.

But those rowdies who sat below his desk,
and under threat of the rounders-bat,
stayed in until the yards clocked off.

Saturday I went that way to the match,
and from the engine-grooves picked bottle-tops
that printed a corona in my soft palm —

the brand of industry I'd later miss.
But now each time I ease off the cap,
the first whiff of that beer takes me back

to those *good footballers* kept behind
to make up for lack of brains by learning
silence, or the art of brewing perhaps.

The Last Barge

The boy is still there
under the redundant mill.
All afternoon he has been watching
the impertinent minnows twitch the float,
its luminous yellow quill-tip deceive
the clasping dragonflies.
But still it does not cock,
begin its thrilling, tipsy run…

and then the grating of the gates,
the water flows back into the lock.
The last barge comes,
carrying hidden cargo under tarpaulins,
an old fox crumpled on the tiller,
and the fox-faced girl,
caught in mid-clamber, staring back
from beneath her coaly thatch.

Too late to follow.
Wait for the chiming laughter,
the sunlit daughters in their first bikinis.
Wait for the pleasure boats.

First Bus

It's a sugar of a frost, not yet morning.
The cattle in the suburban field
lift their heads to me under the sodium.
I've just missed the last game of the gods,

but not the first bus that turns the corner,
a ship of light breaking the crust of the road.
The doors flap open. The driver's deadpan,
the seat still depot-cold.

Unpleasured faces look through me,
a war behind them, a pension-book ahead.
I'm the imposter on the deck.
My jacket ain't leather, not yet.

There's only last night's paper to read.
It's already untrue, like the stop-out moon.
I rub a porthole on the glass.
Griffons glower down from Assurance Street.

Hair tumbling from a hood,
the duffle-coated girl climbs in
(she sorts the letters two rows to my left).
We smile, but haven't yet learnt to speak.

Tyres spit and swish.
I match her footsteps in the frost.
Townboys squint out of yards,
resentful, sucking cigarettes.

Then, like the relaxation of a grip,
I find myself drawing level,
trying hard for my words,
as love's work begins.

On Leaving a Provincial Town

The rear-lights dwindling uphill
into the layered shadow-smoke
stretch out his idea of departure
across a steeplechase of fields,

as the Sunday bells which now begin
tell their traditional version of the evening
in which a sense of village is recalled,
except this is the edge of town,

a town already melted into photographs,
its pavements warming and cooling
through wars and snowfalls and carnivals,
a thousand years, let's say, of history

into which he was suddenly spliced
and yet has no business but to belong,
watching the flashing inter-cities,
the aeroplanes in the hems of sunset.

He's never left, has long since outgrown
the gang smoking under the chestnut tree,
and suffers at dusk the same *farsickness*
that once made hometown boys into soldiers.

Already he dreams himself, the local hero returning,
in the eyes of that beauty who turned him down,
the friend of everyone in both bars, a worthy
of these celebration bells, back for good.

Such boys turn into men one summer evening,
walking out slowly in the sun with prams,
like amateurs still in the Third Round of the Cup,
condemned to wish for nothing but luck.

Last Cafe in the West

In that town you've always passed through
Thinking *What a place to wind up in* —
one day you'll have to stop and try the café,
if only to put its melancholy to the test.

The steamed-up windows warn it's a trap
where the tea's been stewing all summer
and the special menu's left scrubbed blank.
You break the crust on the sugarbowl —

the jukebox fuzzes a Glitter hit,
there's just the waitress playing the fruit-machine
even though she knows it's fixed —
she'll talk to you because you smell of the city.

She wants to get away from here and act,
to leave the local champion practising out back,
she doesn't want to be his girl any more
and turn into the woman in the upstairs flat.

You'd take her too if the last chapter of Angels
didn't burst in, snap the chairs to beating bats
and leave the walls bleeding ketchup,
the waitress love-bitten and her tears unpaid.

You won't defend her — she'll wait for the next,
or take a chance on the soldier from the camp,
after too many vodkas at the dinner-dance,
and get pregnant down a lane in the van.

She only stayed here this long to play a cameo
in the dream you've been filming along this road.
Next time you come looking for the location:
clear glass, antiques, the woman in the upstairs flat,

still in her nightdress, her hair in a mess,
shouting down: *it closed up some summers back*,
as the red lens of the sun pans out on you —
last customer of the last café in the West.

Renaissance Steps

Rising from the reeking shambles,
morning breezes plucking at my sleeves,
I rushed into the cool institutions,
taking the steps in twos and threes.

That was the hour of the new beards,
when talent jingled in its silver spurs,
all the doors above were open,
all the stars were wanderers.

Inside, benefactors pretended
they had worlds at their fingertips,
they twirled their globes hypnotically,
turned my ambitions into ships.

Now I sit among pagodas,
screened by forests of bamboo,
I watch the children's flying rockets
climb into the future blue.

Here the random winds becalmed me,
in the cockpit of my sedentary age,
the stars look through my telescope,
the steps dwindle to a narrow gauge.

The spirit ascends until it enters
the secret uterus of space,
it is reborn upon the idle plateaux
where the giant pandas pace.

The Bull Among the Poppies

All that month a field of poppies
blazed along the road we took to work,
while opposite, in a triangular paddock,
a bull was fattening for the show.

I imagined I was in love. Talking to her
could send a shudder through my bones,
and on the evenings she drove me home
I checked the fields like a proprietor.

That scarlet carpet, that alabaster repose,
were ciphers of something I wished to own
or ancient opposites to be resolved
in myself and in the world.

Halfway home, they broke our conversation
(her daughter's sleeplessness, my poems) —
I imagined her naked body
spread out in the fire glow.

At night, searching in a book,
her scent did not go cold —
Demeter had no husband, I read,
and saw her yellow hair unfurled.

Every day I felt the shudder deepen
and the atmosphere between us grow close,
it was hot and the bull lay down,
the poppies were full-blown.

The moment seemed to approach,
then stand still in the heat, deferred.
The next generation was in love,
we saw them coming through the corn.

July. Mirages waved on the tarmac.
The storm the sky promised was withheld.
The field faded and the bull was shown.
The work became mundane, the road.

When she cleared her desk,
she left me the typewriter.
It shuddered through a sheaf of poems.
They made the fire glow.

Until winter driving the road alone,
an image floated across plain field,
greater than memory, in suspended strength —
the bull among the poppies, cooling, content.

The Roman Returns

His laugh is a coarse intrusion
upon the breathless concubines
spreadeagled on their sumptuous cushions,
surprised amidst orgasmic chimes.

You are fluttering among the doves,
have you forgotten Asclepius' cock?
He returns the standard to their love.
They deftly spring the armour-lock.

The skirt is lifted, the helmet plucked,
they coo sarcastic over battle-sores,
one smooths in oil while the other's fucked,
Why must men make such stupid wars?

The question hangs upon the air,
they stop his answer with their lips,
Venus awards a triumph to the pair,
he can't beat their Babylonian tricks.

The eunuch brings the dripping taper round,
smoke cools through the waterpipes,
mosaics shimmer on a golden ground,
they dream the future archetypes.

The soldier with his sheath of flowers,
the woman with her stiff winter rods,
in dreams put on each other's powers,
self-sufficient as the gods.

No short sword, no stabbing upward thrust,
no conquest, jealousy, or fuss,
it is these dreams we pretend to trust
until the Roman returns in all of us.

If he wakes he'll want to know
what devil taught them while he was away,
he'll drink and smash the painted bowl,
they'll call the lictors and make him pay.

Best then to leave him sleeping, slip out
to tease the boy who stokes the hypocaust,
he says there's a new tribe going about
whose love is genderless, unenforced.

The Man to Trust

At last it's just like the ads,
the dinner's eaten, the coffee's plunged.

She slips away through the partition.
A shy half-smile. The moment has come.

I cradle the brandy-balloon.
Well-being spreads through the room.

Her books and posters approve
my reflection in dark mahogany.

Suddenly she's back, hair re-puffed,
placing herself gingerly in my hands.

It's slim, fresh to the touch —
she knows I am the man to trust:

Will you read this
and tell me what you think?

Fallow

That year he left me fallow
I had grown weary of myself
yielding to the plough and the harvester.
Nobody disturbed me for months.
My ditches swelled then froze.
Foxes came foraging over the snow,
leaving me pocked as the moon.
It was a relief to be empty.

Spring blew in disappointed birds,
the tractors turned my track to mud,
a stallion crashed the one remaining gate.
I rose in weeds and patches then
but hardly showed the summer come
or felt the slither of the snake.
My pair of lovers came to plant their seed,
but found no cover and wound on.

I parched. I cracked. My ditches drained.
Those wavy afternoons of hot mirage
I dreamed of what might one day rise in me,
below, where I slope down to the stream,
an ample house with folded eaves,
a shallow pool where the girls might bathe
among shading trees, and in the trees nests,
and in the nests the birds of heaven.

Autumn. Rested. I waited for him —
that clumsy farmer with his farrow
come to churn me up again,
slop his crop into my rich grooves.
I missed his aimless broadcast corn,
his turnip-head and swede,
even the hay I rolled his daughters in.
But no one came till spring.

Then men who work but do not sing,
exhausting me with silage, kale and rape,
leaving no ditch in which to breathe.
I grow bitter without hedge and gate,
deeper and deeper hide the plan,
determined not to show this generation
the cool villa or the mosaic snake.
Till better grows in them I wait.

The Landscape

When I asked him why he had come,
he said *I have come to repaint the landscape.*
I am rather fond of these old colours, I said.
But he shook his head. *Everything must be repainted.*
I watched him mix the new colours on his palette.
There was midnight black and fiery red.
But they are such simple colours!
The simplest, he said.
I watched him set up his easel.
It towered above us in the sky.
How long will all this take? I said.
Seconds, he said, split-seconds, less.
And then his brush swept the horizon,
obscuring the outline of the hills.
The sky was midnight black,
the earth was fiery red.
He turned to me, his face as grey as lead.
Why did you let me do that? he said.
You could have stopped me,
you saw the colours black and red,
you stood and watched me mix them.
I am an ordinary man, I said,
I do not paint landscapes.
But it was your landscape, he said,
and now your sky is midnight black
and your earth is fiery red
and our faces are grey, as grey as lead.

*3. Eight Gates to the Rain
in the Streets*

Giants

Mother, I'm meeting my nightmares,
the giants that hushed me when you read.
Here is the castle where Giantkiller Jack
came to sever their one two three heads
with the sharp little sword
the Justices of Cornwall lent.
I had to see the pictures before I slept,
just to make sure the giants were dead.

Mother, I've crawled up the beanstalk,
to be in the House of Fear we built back then,
where many last prayers went unheard,
and a sack swung slow on a beam.
Mother, you wished me sweet dreams,
but we never in our wildest thought
I'd end in the place reserved for the frights
which lurked behind every tree.

Mother, I'm meeting the headlines in the flesh,
the ones you wouldn't let me see.
Here is the rabid fiend
who chased me across the foggy heath.
Here are the flabby hands
that squeezed until I couldn't breathe.
Mother I can hear him singing,
and I think he's coming for me.

Shaven bonce, low brow, scowling mien,
now he's here, right in front of me,
the worst of the worst grown tall
the one they could never reprieve.
He wants to know if you're still alive,
and chides me for having no children.
Sometimes he even calls out your name
behind the door, when the lights go out.

Mother, it's safe in here, safer than houses
where I slept as a child and dreamt
of these very men coming to get me,
but it's me who has come to get them,
with the sharp little pen the Justices lent.
Mother, I'm just writing to let you know
I have got inside the book we read
where the beast craves the gentleness you gave me.

The Photographer's Chair

Sit here where every reception's sat
and felt the divider slotted up the crack,
it keeps the body centred and quite still
for long exposure in the County Jail.

The boy who squirmed in pew and desk
was planted in this hard chair to test
his mask against the screw's grimace,
both knowing their unsmiling place.

In Standing Orders 1902 it stands
lips must be licked when the camera commands,
to prevent unnatural expressions of the mouth,
except that chagrin unseen on the out.

That look has not changed, nor the chair,
though laws have come and gone that sat men there,
the shot's still a stigma no mug can avoid,
sat, snapped and quartered now in polaroid.

Recidivists put pebbles in their cheeks,
so constables wouldn't clock them on the streets,
or gurned towards the Ilford Plates
to confound the local magistrates.

Strugglers who didn't want their likeness kept
were sat in cuffs, their faces cupped,
to face the future through the lens
and be forever fixed in their offence.

This is where the soul is stolen for the files,
stapled to reports that Discipline compiles,
to languish in Records with no hope of release,
except to albums well-thumbed by police.

Sit here where every reception's sat
and felt the divider slotted up the crack,
it's your triptych, mate, your life-defining snap,
and, worse still, you'll never get it back.

Midday Bang-up

All the men have gone home.
The prison sweetens the whistle
of the curating ghost
who waits at the inner gate.
This is what it will be like
afterwards, when the light
falls in empty shafts
as if into a Sunday factory.
Every midday the prison issues
its silent ultimatum to the age,
museum, museum, it says, it says.

A Lifer in Summer

Behind the pipes the crickets
rumour the summer permanently,
I think of the sunsets wasted
on those who believe themselves free.

Sunlight is thick on the stagnant canals,
the leaves are trapped on the trees,
inside this failed chrysalis
I ransack my memories.

Someone is having my summer out there
walking through the gap that I leave,
someone is consuming the girl I loved,
my garden is choking with weeds.

I can't put a face to that man
camouflaged against the greens,
his limbs are lost in the branches,
his voice is the rustle of leaves.

Who is it out there in the haze
waving in summer's company?
Is it the life that I took,
or the life you have taken from me?

Offer me more than the smell of the grass
drifting in on the arbitrary breeze,
offer me more than a glimpse of the hill
where you preferred not to hang me.

Invitation to a Cell

The screws are spinning on the Fours,
it's market-day, they've come to peruse
the shoddy bric-a-brac set out
along a line of antique booths,
while the traders hover nervously outside.
Their customers banter, handle, but do not buy.
They've heard the pitches all before.

More than houses cells give the sense
of what someone must look like from inside,
some are hospitable as desert tents
and some as cold as catacombs —
this is beyond the grave alive,
this is the microwave, the fridge,
no telling how each man cooks and cools.

His hookey neighbourhood hands on
the things that can't go on the bus,
the soiled carpet, the light-starved plant,
such comforts a life has cobbled up.
Be his guest, because he has none,
be brave, don't spring the lock,
trust the tea in his one bit of China.

And though you know he'll retell the tale
of wife and kids, and Easy Street long forfeit,
one afternoon like this, he'll confide in you:
the lost two minutes he spent in the red mist…
Yet, even as he's speaking, you'll glimpse
a spectre at his shoulder, mouthing the truth —
his victim, unheard within the prison din.

End of Shift

The inner and outer wickets alternate,
opening and closing like seacocks.
Twice daily this dry dock swells
to hubbub as the key-light screws
await the shout to go ashore.

The roll tallies at twelve o'clock,
the engine in the boilerhouse cuts —
the sense of drifting, control lost,
as with its gate-thunder the prison docks,
divulges the turnkeys to the town.

They try to blend with the streets
but something marks them off,
even to the wife who waits on the estate
with a grudge against the Service
that posts her husband so long away.

She greets him with thin-lipped complaints,
like an inmate twelve hours behind the door.
They'll both do more than life inside;
and he tells you one day, unguarded at the gate:

My daughter wants to be an actress.
Can you help?

Bonfire Night

Like an empty fuel-can
the Nick seeps miasmic mist,
the mirage of its end by fire.
Ask any passing arsonist.

Yet come November, dusk the fifth,
he'll dread the airbombs and to feel
the Bonfire Boys drum up outside
the local version of Bastille.

The procession fizzles in the street.
He fakes his dungeon mask for me.
Next year, I'll see it for myself
or they can throw away the key.

When the roof came off in '68,
he was first among the firebrands,
but if C wing went up tonight
they'd find they have him on their hands,

wedged up, grumpy in his slippers,
with flask and half an ounce of snout,
calligraphing his Christmas cards:
I'm staying put, now you clear out!

Visiting Wives

Are nocturnal on the morning bus, ghost-hybrids,
black-blonde, backcombed, eye-shadowed like stopouts,
hampered by push-chairs and overscolded kids
which may or may not be his. They harbour doubts

and secret parcels of hashish, yeast
to smuggle past the gatelodge in their bras.
This is their abroad, this is their East,
they don't speak the language of the guards

who mouth innuendos behind the glass,
strip-search their bodies with a sidelong glance,
thinking in blue films no censor would pass,
what they'd do to the skirt given half the chance.

She's mule to a man for whom work means crime,
the sex-doll with silver sweets in her kisses.
heavy-petted till the surly screw calls time,
she pretends to preserve what he misses.

But with foul weather comes the decision
that for the kid's sake she could do better.
She admits the wish to keep him in prison,
fixes her hair, posts the undated letter…

Dear John…

Forget-Me-Not

Where everything not issue is traded and sold,
coveted a hundred times over, even the body,
the worst of the waste is the vile paperfold
dropped from barred windows into the gulley.

There's peelings of hooch tipped out in a spin,
when keys came a-jingling down landings,
the remnants of meals from those dining in,
failed slings from window panhandlings.

Grey sock, white knife, puce plate, blue cup,
compose a still life with empty shampoos,
a ripper has left the Jack of Clubs face up
on a murder of linen dumped in the stews.

This is the very bottom of the economy,
the heap no totter would bother to comb,
where even things lose their identity,
ownerless, shapeless, thrown out of home.

Little here then for the dogs to surprise,
nor the gulleyman's spike unclogging the drain,
only the trimmings of denims cut down to size,
a bellyflopped book half-read by the rain.

But when spring sneaks in beneath the wire,
and sun-shafts grill this dismal slope,
a blue mirage hazes over the mire,
out of rottenness grows the flower of hope.

Jackdaws

Their call is nothing short of threat,
these sentries posted on the fence and wall,
not one aspires to be the prisoner's pet,
the escape committee would roast them all.

They clatter in the vacant tower
descending to mess the scraps at twelve,
putting on the strut and peck of power
to show the gulleyman where to delve.

They form the strongest union and control
the motley pigeons in their prison blue,
maintain a constant roof and yard patrol,
as if they owned the place, and they do.

Stroppy, tetchy, full of spite,
left to bicker among the bins,
only years in you realize what might
be reincarnated in their wings —

the portly constable unfit for town
the hapless chaplain mocked by the pews,
the sour schoolman in his fraying gown,
the grizzled turnkey turning the screw.

No doubt these prison types recur,
you pass them daily in the glooming halls;
beware! the prison jackdaws caw,
the poet's the worst malcontent of all.

The Prison Cricket

I am the conscience of this keep,
even when there is privacy to dream,
it will not let you sleep.

Dry symphonies of friction seep
from the old brick's crumbling seam,
I am the conscience of this keep.

I tense my twin antennae, bleep
the signal the vagrant dead still beam,
it will not let you sleep.

Even though no judas-eye can peep
into the futures that you scheme,
I am the conscience of this keep.

When the futile broom comes to sweep
the stale light the morning can't redeem,
it will not let you sleep.

I am the itch of hopes that creep
upon your flesh, the faintest gleam,
I am the conscience of this keep,
it will not let you sleep.

Child of the Prison

Some days he's mingling with Visits,
rolling a marble in the groove of the gate,
or sat on the step of the lodge,
like a scolded boy told to wait.

Some nights a screw on F wing
answers a phantom bell for the bog,
or, sauntering back from a pegging,
finds his page turned in the log.

Sometimes he's with the Grey Lady,
tousling the curls on his head,
surrogate for the still-born baby
they ghosted from her infirmary bed.

Tonight he's the mouse at bang-up,
scuttling out as I'm whistling past:
I am half-sick of spooking the prison.
Won't you go out and father me at last?

Maundy Thursday on the Exercise Yard

The Sussex Light Blues are on parade,
still obeying the drill of the system,
treading anti-clockwise by tradition
of the regiment willing to enlist them.

Crimes are castes, as fixed as professions,
and, though no one is here for display,
they walk at the pace of aldermen,
in the only blue hour of their day.

Don't mess with the gym-toned gangster
with the carpet-rolls under his arms,
he's studied the scowl which blanks you,
but that is the least of his charms.

Cutting capers one pace behind him,
trying to please like the fool of a king,
his gofer dances attendance —
it's a co-dependency thing.

Lifers are loners, they keep well apart,
their gaze never lifts from the ground,
they acquire the sureness of judges
as the years go round and round.

Holy Joe has a cross above his bed,
walks under the weight of his halo,
but he killed an innocent girl in Kent,
just on the Devil's say-so.

Now limps the untouchable gulleyman
followed by the scruffiest of crows,
as if the very birds had learnt to peck
in the order of these rotten rows.

This hopeless circle is the prison trope
wherein spook treadmill, crank and screw.
It inclines the mind to stick by the old,
urges reform — to re-invent the new.

The Shadow Board

Seven years of cancelled windows
and feathers ingrown for the Great Escape,
you tricked the secret of flight
from the pigeons protesting on the slates.

Strange you broke out of the Chapel
chose the wall by the gallows-ground,
your body pending on the razor-wire
swinging above the promised town.

They found your shadow on the shadow board
and spun the wing out of the dark,
but the dummy strung up in your cell
kept mum in your seven-year mask.

No guvner, no screw and no grass
could have known what you wanted so much.
Somewit put a note from you in the box —
Won't be long just gone for a fuck.

But the buzz of being out there
will go like your last line of whizz —
and the virgin killer riding his luck
will find out what a prison that is —

Where everyone's re-reading your story
and your name's on the tip of their tongue,
where you're always checking the windows
and you can't go shadowless into the sun.

On your door it still says NO TRAY,
but Somewit's added NO RICKY,
one off guv, he taunts the landing-screw,
but they all want you back and quickly.

Not safe with one of their number out there,
after all the time they've invested,
you have become the stuff of their dreams
they'd rather not really see tested.

Ricky, no one in here will give you odds
now you've stolen back your own body,
but I hope you find one helluvafuck
before the running gets rocky.

Seven years of cancelled windows
in canary-stripes Nowit finds funny,
they'll knock you back on the shadow board,
then let out the mask and the dummy.

On the Doors of B Wing

UNDER NEW MANAGEMENT, it says,
but the diesel's as bad as before,
BE THANKFUL FOR SMALL MERCIES,
there's no longer blood on the floor.

KNOCK TWICE AND ASK FOR WENDY,
if you knock only once it's Dave,
for half an ounce or a decent puff
he'll let you into her cave.

Make no mistake, THE WALRUS lives here,
likes them big-arsed, big-titted,
right now he's over the hospital,
getting a new tusk fitted.

This is PETER's PETER
the bard who gazes starwards,
the angels inspire him to write,
THE MET ARE ALL BENT BASTARDS.

PLEASE DON'T ASK FOR CREDIT
even when you bust your spends,
cos Harry'll tell you just like Harry
A REFUSAL OFTEN OFFENDS.

STEVE OF WHITEHAWK doing a five,
the Chaplain thinks he's funny,
because on the card outside his cell
against RELIGION he's scribbled MONEY.

This was SMITH THE MASTERBREWER
Whose hooch was deemed a godsend,
but now he's GONE TO WAYLAND,
passed pissed into Lewes legend.

Always tell Tricky Ricky's door
Because it used to say NO TRAY.
now they've added AND NO RICK
since he upped and had it away.

This one's LITTLE JOE'S DEN,
don't you ever go in and forget it,
I'm the millionaire next door
NEMO ME IMPUNE LACESSIT.

Col saw the hand against the wall
that wrote THE CHRIST IS RISEN,
but no one knows who wrote below
NOT YET IN THIS FUCKING PRISON.

If He came back and lived on B wing,
He'd write in blood above His door,
DAD HOW COME YOU LEFT ME?
or LOVE DON'T LIVE HERE ANY MORE.

A Laugh in the Hospital

The helpful redband informs you at the door,
the doctor's the one in the white coat.
There's always been laughter in this ward,
hysteria as common as a sore throat.

No longer debtors, now the senile and insane
are detained in this cushy ward of the prison.
Yet overbrimming will bring the syringe,
straight waistcoat, pending expert decision.

King Cocaine suffers ridicule on the throne,
waiting to pass his swallowed stash;
the barber's razor trembles with the irony,
as it shaves the sectioned psychopaths.

In here you meet more relatives of the Queen
than you would at a weekend in Balmoral,
men who bring down lightning and hurricanes
with whom it's inadvisable to quarrel.

Who brought such wild infection in —
the amputee perhaps, gone merry in his ether,
the Second Christ nutted off from the wing,
the tweeny tickled to death by her fever?

Or perhaps the surgeon, consulting his chart,
the day they put the crazed navvy away —
From Ireland are you, Michael? Which part?
All of me, doctor, like your bloody railway.

Spends

When there's an off a posse comes pounding,
a Rembrandt of screws in the light-dark hall,
an anonymous body has crashed from the landing,
the net on the Twos has broken its fall.

A carpet of claret is fitting the recess,
Nobody's toothbrush is sporting a blade,
Somebody's face is looking a mess
for leaving his canteen bill unpaid.

When it comes on top it's usually money,
the nick's just economics writ small,
but when you go bust you pay with your body
if you don't block yourself or go over the wall.

If you've got a habit and no more spends,
prison's one hell of a hell to be,
where even the Devil worships whoever lends
and not even *good morning* is free.

A habit inside gets harder to break,
though there's no head stronger than mine,
a head never knows how much it can take,
till it's slugged with a sock of PP nine.

So if you go into prison, don't go into debt,
that's the only advice a body can give,
a grey bag is all that a body will get
when it deals in prison to live.

A Quiet Day in the County Gaol

Billy's putting in an app.
cos he wants his harmonica back,
they took it away when he played a snatch
of *Train Time* to the circuit judge
just before he weighed him off
and put him on the bus down here.

Last Friday it was fish, always is,
only Harry put his up on the ceiling
shouting *Pick the bones out of that!*
He always had a bit of a temper Harry,
his wife could have told you as much
till he put his hands round her neck —
it must have been her fish, I guess.

In here, murder's common-or-garden,
not pump-action psychopathic stuff.
The lifers like to keep it simple mid-career.
Take Dickie for example. He likes a rakker
over tea and civvies in the afternoon.
Sometimes the stars themselves drop in,
cos Dickie once stood a drink to Jack the Hat.

The mice are moody, the alert is amber,
rumour is we're getting back the prison cat,
Chav says I should bring in a ferret,
we'll keep it kushti, under wraps.
Recently he's hit a level patch — is happy
so long as by bang-up he's got a puff
and batteries if the wall's not wired up —
but he still cries most nights behind the door
listening to some sad cat blow the sax.

The hooch bubbles in the fire-extinguishers,
the crickets counterpoint the clocks.
It's been a quiet day in the County Gaol.
Shhh. Shhh. The past is seeping back like gas.

The mice skitter. Enter the ghost of the prison cat.
She stops and tilts her head to catch
a sound that's warming in the belly of the Nick.
There is a sense of turning shafts and cranks,
a heavy engine just beginning to move —
Train Time — Billy's got it back.

Suspendatur

The boy arrives before his beard,
awards himself thin soup, no prayers,
befriends the screws who parent him, it's weird
to think he might have been one of theirs.

Same silence that drove the oakum-pickers mad,
plaits the noose around his neck,
let's hope the men who hanged his great granddad
will catch him before he hits the deck.

Spots, borstal dots and stitched wrists,
he bears the markings of past candidates,
they move him off YPs, because the M.O. insists,
to the ward that's furthest from his mates.

His file gets stamped forever with an F,
he's put on watch, but the log's a sham.
One man, one cell can equal death,
when, like tomb-slabs, the bang-ups slam.

The bolts and bars man finds him at unlock
naked, pendant from the window-slit.
No mouth-to-mouth, nor pads can shock
him back to the death-in-life he quit.

Ask the oakum-pickers in the sunless wards.
They'll tell you as they unpick the rope,
on the solitary the shadow falls inwards,
into the soul, beyond the pale of hope.

The Copper Beech

For the abstract Time read Tree,
the one that's waited outside the gate
a hundred years, shading the patience
of wives and mothers early for Visits.

It houses unnoticed creatures,
whose world it is, and who hatch
no plans beyond their nests,
no days beyond this day.

In a year, if you watch, it'll teach
to darken in the midday sun,
to hang like the caterpillar hangs
in its branches by a thread.

In five, come summer, you'll know
each frill of its burgundy dress,
then envy the squirrel and its store,
snug within the autumn trunk.

In ten you'll have moved away
to a window with just a wall to tell
she died or left like they always do.
Not one of them can be trusted.

And when they let you out on licence
crushed in your winter-grey suit,
the only one there at the gate
will be the tree, having served alongside,

grown taller while you grew small,
too magnificent in the breeze,
but still waiting for someone
who used to be you.

The Last Man Out

On the closure of C wing

The prison wears grey weather well,
drips with its proper melancholy then —
bedraggled jackdaws share the alcoves
of barred windows that still imply the men.

But they have gone, the wing is dead,
pre-empts the day this place will close
and stand abandoned like a factory
when the final hooter blows.

I find myself on empty landings
wondering who'll be the last one out of here,
and if, as the bulldozers move in,
he'll feel impelled to make its ending clear

and improvise the ultimate gesture to seal
this harrow and this haven of the poor —
not the clenched fist, nor the V-sign,
nor the tag sprayed on the door,

but the open palm, the privilege denied inside
of giving, something natural and unbound —
a handful of grass to the sun-dappled horse,
restoring its grazing rights to this ground.

Eight Gates to the Rain in the Streets

Your smell is under my skin,
I am branded with your tattoos.
When you opened up your gate,
you did not set me loose.

Long after I've gone from you,
I still dream out the keys.
Square key, round key,
square key, round key...

Underneath the leaden sky,
I am imprisoned still,
'What is freedom?' asks the bird,
flying from the sill.

Long after I've gone from you
It's still your flint and brick I see.
square key, round key,
square key, round key...

I can't open a door without you,
leave it unlocked for long.
Your bars cross every window.
I cross off the years to come.

Long after I've gone from you,
I still taste your metal in my tea.
Square key, round key,
square key, round key...

I miss you like my mother,
I miss you like my school,
and I am ashamed to say
I miss the prison rule.

Long after I've gone from you,
I still dream out the keys,
Square key, round key,
square key, round key...

Eight gates to the rain in the streets.

A Glossary of Prison Terms

app - a written application to see a governor grade, a doctor, teacher, etc.

bang up - lock up time, but also the time spent daily locked in the cell.

behind the door - in the cell, the time a prisoner is alone in his cell.

block - the punishment cells for disciplinary offences and for Rule 43s.

body - the dehumanising term for a prisoner used by a prison officer when handing him over to another member of staff.

Borstal dots - dotted tattoos on the finger and knuckle to show that a boy has done time in Borstal.

canary-stripes - more often known now as 'patches'. These are yellow stripes in the trousers previous or potential escapees are forced to wear so that they can be easily recognized by staff.

civvies - manufactured cigarettes, as opposed to prison roll-ups, but also civilians working in prison.

claret - blood.

deps - depositions, the details of an inmate's court-case. He is allowed to have copies of these.

diesel - prison tea.

dining in - eating meals on a tray in the cell. Dining out, in large canteens, has been largely abandoned in British prisons, owing to control problems.

double - when prison gates are secured for the patrol state at night, or for special security, they are locked with a second key, a 'doubles key'. This is called 'doubling'. You can be 'doubled in' if you are caught behind one of these gates without a doubles key.

E man - a previous or potential escapee.

firm - a crew of 'gangsters' who will assume authority over a landing or possibly a wing. The staff will respect this hierarchy as well as the inmates.

five - as in 'he's doing a five', i.e. a five year sentence.

forty-three - a sex offender can opt under Rule 43 to place himself in the segregation unit to protect himself from attack from other prisoners.

Fours - the wings of most Victorian gaols are divided into three or four landings. These become universally known as the Ones, the Twos, the Threes, The Fours. These are used to identify locations.

gangster - a hard man on the wing who is physically and financially in control of its market, usually part of a 'firm'.

gatelodge - the lodge between the outer and inner gates at the front of a prison. A world in itself.

ghost - suddenly to move an inmate to another prison, often at night, and without his consent. 'Where's Ken? He's been ghosted'.

gulleyman - arguably the worst job in the prison, cleaning out the gulleys below the windows of the wings, where rubbish and excrement is often dropped.

half-ounce - of tobacco which is sold in half-ounces from the prison canteen. It is the most common form of currency in prison.

have it away - to escape.

home leave - longterm prisoners are given several spells in the outside world during the final year of their sentence.

hooch - illicit alcohol brewed in prison.

hotplate - the steel oblong where the food is served on the wing in the 'dining in' system.

Judas - the Judas eye, the spy-hole in the cell-door, now more commonly a flap than a hole but still referred to as 'the Judas'.

landing - Victorian prisons are divided into wings and landings. A landing can have an atmosphere of its own, quite separate from the one above or below it. The landing, not the wing, is often a man's community in prison.

licence - a life sentence is for life. Though a lifer may serve perhaps fifteen years or even less, he is then only released on a licence, which can be revoked by the Home Office at any time.

location - description of a prisoner's wing, landing and cell number.

lost two minutes - during my time at Lewes I heard many lifers speak of 'the lost two minutes', covering the actual moment their crime was committed, which they claim cannot be recalled.

mid-career - a lifer is said to be in mid-career after he has served the first four years of his sentence and settled down in a training prison for example the lifers unit in Lewes.

M.O. - Medical Officer.

moody - dubious, but can perversely mean very good in some contexts.

MUFTI - Minimum Use of Force for Tactical Intervention, used to break hostage-situations, riots, clean-up operations in a prison.

mule - a carrier of drugs, usually a female visitor.

nonce - a sex offender. **nonced off** - to be driven into segregation on Rule 43 by pressure from fellow inmates.

note in the box - on each wing there is a box for applications, but this is also used for grassing anonymously to the staff. It is therefore used by inmates with great circumspection.

no tray - after dining in, trays are left outside the cell for collection. Those who work in the prison kitchen also eat there. They put this sign up on their cell door to indicate they are not dining in.

off - an off, a fight, a riot, all occasions when the alarm is pressed.

on the bus - moved to another prison.

on the out - out of prison, in the outside world.

on top - when the pressure is becoming too great on an inmate, or when he is about to be caught for something, or a situation is about to explode, he will say 'it's coming on top'.

one off - one off the roll. An officer might shout this when taking a 'body' out of a wing or unit controlled by another member of staff. Conversely, **one on** - when handing an inmate over to another officer.

parcel - a deal of marijuana or yeast brought in by a visitor. But also a shit-parcel dropped through the bars into the gulley below the wing.

pegging (or **pegging in**) - similar to clocking on. Every twenty minutes on night-duty an officer must peg in to a rotating time-disk to show that he is still awake. This cardboard disk can be removed and checked by his seniors at the end of the night-shift.

peter - a cell.

puff - marijuana.

rakker - Romany for a long session of talk, a natter.

recess - the wash-basins and toilets on the wing are housed in the recess. Out of sight of the staff, it is the usual venue for violence.

redband - a trusted, responsible prisoner who is allowed to move more freely within the prison.

remand - a prisoner awaiting trial. Some men can serve over a year on remand.

roll - the number of prisoners held in the prison at any particular time. It is checked several times a day.

seg - the segregation unit, used for 43s and as the punishment block.

shadow board - In prison all tools and utensils are hung on a board painted with their black shadow-images so that it can quickly be ascertained when one is missing.

Silent Rule - until the First World War prisoners were held in prison in silence, and were not allowed to communicate with each other, only with members of staff.

snout - Tobacco. Sometimes also salmon, as in 'salmon trout', rhyming slang for 'snout'.

spends - the weekly amount a prisoner may spend at the canteen. He may augment his paltry wages with private cash.

spin - a cell-search. There is a statutory requirement to search prisoners' cells regularly.

spur - New Model Prisons were designed with spurs radiating off a central hub, the Centre, from where all the wings could be observed.

Standing Orders - directives from the Home Office establishing practice within prisons.

Suspendatur - *Latin*. 'Let him be hanged'. In capital cases before the nineteenth century the Clark of the Court at the East Sussex Assizes would write this in the ledger when the offender was to be hanged.

sweet key - a non-security key that locks unimportant rooms in the prison.

tally - the brass disc worn on the key-chain by staff when they are outside the prison gate. It bears the number of their set of keys.

Verne - H.M.P. The Verne on Portland Bill near Weymouth, a category C prison to which many of the lifers from Lewes, a B category prison, graduated.

V.O. - a visiting order which must be sent in advance by a prisoner to his visitor.

wedge up - a wooden wedge is used to stop intruders or staff bursting into a cell uninvited. The one means of obtaining privacy in prison outside of bang-up.

weigh off - to be sentenced to prison by the judge.

wing - at Lewes the wing comprises four landings, the main wings A and B and C radiate from the Centre.

Works - the agency in the prison responsible for repairs, painting etc.

YP - young prisoner.

4. Tending the Hop

Siren

At the first roar I turned
and left the labyrinths,
slowly retraced my steps
to streets where ever since

I've spoken in my beer
to anyone who'd care
to listen to a life
that almost came to dare.

You'd think sea-perils
and monstrosities of fate
would never visit a man
who stays behind the gate.

But lost among my books,
one night I turned a page,
and deep inside my head
a rock began to rage.

And in that flash I saw
the gleaming megalith,
a glinting limb of granite
perched on the ox-red cliff.

The face I would have seen,
had I sailed the Seven Seas,
the beauty that lies beyond
the Pillars of Hercules.

The voice I would have heard,
had I stayed out on the deck,
the heart-cry of creation
for those who risk their neck.

Now she comes some nights,
to stand before the mast,
preening future feathers,
tarring me with past.

The gaze is undeceived,
without compromise,
I read what I'd have written
brilliant in her eyes.

Know yourself, know yourself,
the oracles pretend,
wisdom is its own reward,
but, traveller, append:

If you stay in Ithaca,
beneath Penelope's wing,
the siren will destroy you
though you never hear her sing.

Grünewald's Madonna

I met you once where the track forks away down to a stream,
your geese honking round after the yellow corn.
The air was hot and close, the afternoon bruising for storm.
You smiled, offered an egg from your basket,
a little salt in a scarlet kerchief,
then watched me eat, holding my gaze with your own,
as long and clear as a mare, until I was done.

The further I travelled on, the clearer you became;
and stopping in Aschaff, awaiting my fee,
I thought my way back to the hay-sweet stable,
to the run of curls at the nape of your neck,
your eyes rolling up to quarter moons
when the angel cried out of you — *Herrgott vergibt!*
as the rain beat down on the empty stalls.

In the Stift, with the fine brush, when I at last began,
I felt your slender fingers guiding my hand,
choosing the ochres of the pomegranate, the lilywhites,
till purple, snow and rainbow made Our Lady complete.
One holy day, I wish, you might happen upon this,
see the smiling child, as ours imagined, and know
how, with all my colours, I repaid your wayside gift.

The Hop Exchange

There is craft in these wrought-iron flowers,
their stems curling around the slender gates.
Did my grandfather pass through here,
tweeded, bristling, beetroot-faced,
having made a packet on the chequered floor?
Did he stand smoking on these steps
taking in the salmon evening,
fingering the trousered cash?

Did he ignore the whistle of the last train west
and wonder instead how London might entertain him
with its secret stairs and gaslit traps?
A three-star dinner, brandy balloons
in the comfort of some half-licensed saloon,
before being led through the drapes
to the silk stockings and the gartered legs,
waiting in the red-flocked room beyond.

Or did he think, as I think back, ahead,
and picture me upon these steps
in my lightweight summer threads
two generations off the farm?
Don't begrudge me my pleasures
you prying scribbler yet unborn
who never sold a pinch of barley.
I'll leave enough for you to waste…

How still the yards must be tonight,
the vines green-golden in the copper sun,
the spires driven up through the horizon like red nails,
showing where our dead are buried.
There is the land we sowed and sold
in exchange for this, my outlandish living,
musing while city men talk money,
and words go for nothing in everyone's beer.

Tending the Hop

Up the ladder, training the runners to the string,
the sudden match of hop-green
against the blue brings a memory,
retrieved from further back
beyond my own lights —
an ancestor sounded out
deep down in the mush.

Read him up. Thomas Parry,
dead at thirty-one, his epitaph:
'under his care the cultivation
of the apple and the hop
was materially improved in the County.
He was a good master,
much respected and liberal to the poor.'

Memorials speak well of the dead,
especially when cut young,
but this legacy already makes mine
feel small, enclosed at fifty-two,
the tenant of a local tongue,
driving my beasts to market,
when the market's already done.

The farm was sold a generation back,
the hop-yards lie under subsidy,
while I buy my beer from the shop,
sit and watch the sliding of events
beyond control, left to those
who serve the money and the lie,
that is (or do I sell short?) the modern lot.

My hop's ornamental, like my business, Tom,
and maybe I've squandered your legacy
by just stringing these words along,
but in those dusty days, patrolling the rows,
listening to the sunbrown girls holler,
filling their baskets up there in the sun,
didn't you, for a moment, imagine
you might one day write all this down?

In the Flax Field

Over the last stile before the station —
a fading blue carpet down to the stream —
flax — antique crop of the papermakers.
I started on the footpath imagining
lost Junes and the heaven it must have been
for lovers who came here once
and chose this place for their coupling.

Halfway across, a plump balloon
in brilliant panelled polyesters
cleared the glossy stand of trees.
It hung in the evening air, then fired up
and drifted disdainful on its way,
leaving me landlocked in the field,
caught between my thoughts and its going.

For this, was it really for this
the cottagers stooped over the plough,
and the field-girls embraced the corn
cutting and binding till they bled?
Just so Lord Leisure might one day
rise up in his ample basket
to survey the country they had made?

No sooner asked than I stumble across
the lovers lying in the flax four centuries back.
He's snoring, after the fact.
She's gazing upwards at the hills,
wondering why the rainbow,
so vivid when they crossed the stile,
leaves no trace in all this blue.

Those Under Saturn

Those under Saturn
stand in the shadows,
while the dance stamps.

Watchers are lovers,
but love chooses others
wherever it tramps.

One turn of the tide,
one shift of the stars,
the raven decamps,

then I'll walk you home,
guided by Venus,
the lighter of lamps.

One Street Back

The young are cooking on the beach.
Time, old friend, to join the bodies
that no longer admire themselves.
Defect from pleasure, past the griddles
and the red-eyed parrot lost for words.
Find a place where you are not overlooked,
where grievances are nursed in a glass,
the job, the girl just missed,
the ball that never crossed the line,
the one that might have turned it all around.

The world's plain one street back.
But hard not to imagine those guys gathered
round the table under the iron lamp,
are none other than the dog-jowled Fates,
hastily concealing plans in long pouches,
the portions of agony they allot to those
who loll under the coconut shades.
Maybe with the courage of three cognacs
you might sway over, offer them a drink,
hoping to catch a glimpse of what's in store.

After four, there's worse to come —
the thought that this is all unplanned,
these men no more than strangers
laying plans for property or crime, or both,
with no purpose beyond the tick of money,
and the heat of their appetencies.
What if the sun has no divinities,
moon metaphors are meaningless?
What if the future is random
except the burn-out of the stars?

The fifth will take the edge off nothingness,
and perhaps by then, if you persist,
the Fate you least expect,
the foxy one with the cicatrix,
will lurch across to join you,
cocking an eye like a pirate,
downing his dram, and only then
revealing in a gnarled fist
the contraband of the impossible —
a single angel-feather floating on his palm.

Serpentine

By the time we breakfast in the yard,
the chisel would have chipped
half the morning away.
It's the same swallow-rented sky,
the same clouds ghosting off the sea,
but now the rubble's laid to flowerbeds.

The children fizz by on wheels,
coming into their own.
One brings the treasure he has found,
a smooth round cast-off end
fitting the palm of his hand —
Any good?

For one brief generation this stone
filled a showroom in the Strand.
Serpentine was once the man,
but even as the hammers rang
along the Lizard, the locals knew
how quickly strands the tide.

By afternoon, the yard is mine.
Above, the martins dip and glide.
I turn, return the obstinate lines,
crossing, cutting to an inner shape,
till the cracks spring and divide.
Chuck it on the pile, begin again, again…

The sky clears.
The jackdaws settle in the thatch.
An hour passes, butterflies, the breeze,
the round end holds the papers down.
At last the shape's defined. I look up.
Any good? asks the turner resting in the shade.

The Acid Bottles

I spent my Sundays in the factory-yards,
playing beneath God's sizzling pylon,
hiding from Him in the bushes beside the pond.
I rubbed portholes in the nicotine-yellowed panes
to gaze into the forbidden Temple of Work,
with its lethal splitting machines,
its monumental, man-crushing drums.
The yards oozed with the sweetness of acetone,
I stirred the oily puddles with my stick,
but I never touched the acid bottles,
the Devil's empties standing straw-packed
outside the drum-room door, reeking sourly in the sun.

But later when I became a man and slept
in disenchanted cities full of voices,
I dreamt that I crept back into those yards,
crossed that scabby, oil-pocked floor
to drink with the Devil in the drum-room.
Together we grasped the rainbow flasks,
downed them in reckless draughts,
desecrating the Temple, blaspheming its absent God.
We danced upon the quivering catwalks
and span inside the runaway drums,
I laughed and laughed, but when I tried to speak,
I tasted the acid on my tongue.

Now, if ever I get back to the factory-yards,
it is the middle of the day,
the workers are sitting beside the pond,
feeding the trusting sparrows their crumbs.
The bushes are heavy with oranges
(as I drew them once in bright crayon).
The boilersuited foreman waits with the bottle,
beckons me between the tumbling drums.
It's too loud to speak. I hand him the phial,
and, smiling, without spilling a drop,
he dispenses the brilliant inks I need
to write of home with irony and love.

Manifest Destiny

Day breaks before the pioneers —
the sunlight still empty of the dust,
the bees trading under the waterfall.

Up the trail, a pair of moccasins
padding the needle carpet underfoot,
come to a silent stop.

First the wafting stink of horse,
then the squeak, squeak, squeak
of the overloaded wheel.

Fresh pine seeps in under the canvas,
the chortle of the creek,
pa whistling *Londonderry Air*.

Below her head the pillow's hard —
the leather book she'll teach,
to raise the savage above the beasts.

She throws off the chintz curtains
from back east, unlaces the flap,
pokes her head out over the tailboard

to see her first pupil, sunkissed,
pissing in a generous golden arc,
marking where the schoolhouse should stand…

Six generations on, her great grand niece
comes backpacking down this trail,
with noiseless moccasins on her feet.

The rock accommodates, the creek chortles on,
the bees trade under the waterfall,
now for this week's assignment: *Chief Joseph Speaks*.

At Licton Springs

The natives have been driven off, but not the gods.
They tremble in leaf, nod in branch,
rooted round this poisoned spring
where once red feet stamped the eagle dance.

Instead, a broken junkie and his squaw,
horse-blankets bundled in a shopping cart,
wait out the noisome day,
backs turned to the adventure park.

This ochre mud once healed,
while the shaman raved beneath his hood,
now a teacher preaches the sacred planet,
with enthusiasm and two planks of wood.

The great grandchildren of the braves
hang listless on the swings, no whoop at all,
waiting on the next full moon,
their monthly visit to the mall.

The Sun Machine

This is where it must be kept,
down streets where the sun comes unsaluted
into coach corrals and loading bays,
ducks into arches, shafts along the gap
between the depot and the trampled fence.

They hid it in this ordinariness —
the last of the enthusiasts
who prized each second of the light.
I blink against as I enquire
among the squinting tribe of gardeners.

One brings the key and leads me
sullen to a garage, springs a lock.
The door is raised on pillars of dust.
beneath the mildewed wraps he shows me
the sunburst on the chrome.

Does it still work? He shrugs.
There's instructions on the back
but no one down here can make head nor tail...
He'd never guess what price a fool
would pay to get his summers back.

But how to move it? Try the phone-box.
It pings like a microwave.
I wait for the pick-up truck.
More lost moments of the sun
are squandered on this cabbage-patch.

I'm haggling in a greenhouse
when the commotion starts —
a throwback with a monkey-wrench
has got it working and, like a turkey,
is strutting the first steps.

Children quick as lizards
slip out between the house-cracks,
they stare into its glowing heart —
it opens, presents a disc and flips,
sending out the message from a dying star:

...but there ain't no cure for the summertime blues...

Urban Fox

Too uncurious for a cat.
His long elastic stretch down the wall
gives him away, and the trot
away from my foreshadow.

He has the talent to adapt,
the country boy made good,
making a decent living
off other creatures' scraps.

Now the terrace has been cleared,
he's slum landlord of the patch,
foraging among the garden flats,
finding cover in a scrubby gap

from where he watches me pass,
bags slung on both shoulders,
early, strange, leaving my habitat,
sniffing a new vixen across the valley.

5. Eden II

Midsummer Moon

Somehow I know we are looking
out at the same moon tonight.
Two thousand years ago, Amaryllis,
I ditched these lines, used the light
to race over the open fields,
for an hour under your eyes.

Now I can only dream you inside this vine,
back an overgrown run of summers,
on such a still, moth-kissed night,
your shoulders oiled, tresses unskeined,
the secret finger to your lips,
slipping from the feast into the corn.

Weave me that myrtle-garland again,
call me poet as you drain the jug
of ruby wine you fetched out for us then.
We were just hours and villages apart,
but those are years and cities now,
and the moon lights the miles and miles.

Just Before

As the pigeon stalls
at the top of its climb,
before swooping low again,

as the raindrop beads
at the tip of the leaf
before it falls away,

as the hare stops,
lifts a paw, ears cocked,
testing the air for danger,

so I hesitate to call you.
Can this restraint
be sweeter than our meeting?

Ask the drinker
as the wine
rubies the bottle's neck.

Ask the smith
as the white iron
shines over the cooling trough.

Ask me
when I hear the triple knock
and know you've found the address.

A Return to Mithymna

Although I sat down to drink with you,
the woman who led me away
from the roar of the brandy-tables
knew these twisting streets too well —

she looked back once, cocking her head,
then sprang up the recession of steps
with a laugh that resembled yours,
only an octave more cruel.

Does she often rent this room?
Does she always choose this bed?
With one throw of her golden belt,
can she borrow another flesh?

The lacquered nail beckons,
moves down the belly like a boat.
The eyes turn upwards, to almonds,
gazing elsewhere, long ago…

When she cried out I heard
the keening of the harbour cats,
shutters closed in quick succession,
then voices raised behind them.

And though it was you I woke with,
your smile still seemed to know
the repertoire of shameful acts
she lived through us last night.

The way the *yayas* look at you today
as you hang the sheets up in the sun,
is half desire, half contempt.
The one they'd driven out is back.

The Spark

As the southering plane wraiths behind cloud,
I picture you from my signal-failed train,
gliding through airport lounges, leaving a trail
of lipsticked cups, flirted magazines, torn stubs.

Travel flatters expectations, makes them wild.
How deeply, in transit, men mourn their lives!
What glances you collect, what subtle darts,
before the first cab sweeps you out of sight…

as the sliding doors bleat and divide.
The aisle does its best to find its feet;
more late angries pack inside
and someone shouts: *Move down please!*

…while the foyer mirror admires your arrival.
The lift rolls back its concertina gates.
The room has perfumed and prepared itself.
Curtains swish on cityscape.

You slip between the silken sheets
with the relief of the unchosen concubine.
Time now for the book postponed,
the anticipations of the heart…

What could I offer you instead
from the cheap tartan seats of second class?
Only this: the City of Light is nothing
to the spark your eyes once threw me in Eden.

In Verona Perhaps

The campanile rings the quarter hours.
The last heels click over the cobblestones.
In what far off city
do you lay down your head tonight?

We are countries apart, and ever have been,
but what if the speeds of hearts and minds
had not divided us back then,
what lives we might have led.

Or is love's power stored longest in unexplored events?
Were we to risk them now,
what bell-bright mornings, what soft goodnights
could we so late append?

The moon fights shy behind the clouds.
Yet one more footfall stalls beneath your window —
Romeo, perhaps, reliving his first attempts,
Orpheus, pining for his receding bride,

or just my dreaming shade,
come to light a candle
at the altar of Venus,
styling your name in the supple wax.

Stained Glass

When the sermon's logic falters,
my gaze begins to drift aloft
to contemplate the great east window,
the centre lancet, below the holy stuff,

where tremulous Adam stands conflicted
to find his nakedness fired up,
while Eve attends the scarlet serpent
corkscrewing round the know-all trunk.

Were that glass now set in modern leads,
we might see post-coital Adam glum,
with Eve puzzling some distance off
why it was she took the plunge.

Didn't the fruit of knowledge
already comprehend all this,
and the dullness of the mind that comes
once desire's wet work is done?

Yet knowing this would not deter me
from risking exile once again,
to learn the ruse the serpent taught her,
passed down to you, my forbidden one.

The Notebook

The hour before we meet still drags,
held back by weight of expectation.
I'm three-quarters early, with notebook, pen,
amidst the barlights of the discreet saloon.

The shuffle selects the random tracks,
recalling the decades of failed romance...
The door awaits your cautious steps...
The dark oak anticipates your portrait...

And as I wait, I picture you,
smoothing the stockings to your legs,
settling on the pearls with that dress
no poet worth the candle would forget.

The pencil lines the eyelids.
The brush makes one more pass.
Your reflection's in no hurry
to break the cab driver's heart.

The hand quickens past the hour.
At last the notebook starts to click:
Take your time, let me savour
the last moments of your lateness.

At the Florist's

Not the cheapskate miniatures,
nor the blowsy top of the range —
these, called freedom, best describe
the potential we hold closed inside.

The assistant takes down addresses,
as if we were complicit in a crime
(it's true - I've walked to the city limits
where my money won't be recognized).

But, rather than reproach, all at once
she blushes up, her eyes shining
with the excitement of the plan,
as if I wooed all womankind.

Even the one 'who takes the orders'
is suddenly flushed with the bold esprit,
and for that moment we're all three inspired
by this custom of nameless tributing

to think of a morning doorstep,
the bell ringing through a quiet hall,
then bare feet padding on the stair,
a peeping face from sleep surprised.

In my mind, of course, it's you,
in theirs, a memory of high-hearted youth,
an expectation that in age survives
of being, for someone, the most loved alive.

Lovelight

Was it the sunlight that gilded Eve
when smiling she retrieved the core,
or Adam's now salacious gaze
honeying the object of his desire?

Was it torchlight and the tambourines
that lent Cleopatra her special lustre,
or Anthony's goggling expectation
of how the passion of the East might blaze?

I saw that gleam again last night
when you drew yourself up on the divan,
and your naked flesh shone iridescent,
beyond the power of any lamp.

Is this the mischievous lovelight
Venus brought with her from the foam?
Is this the veil of appearance that drove the sage
to seek solace in the mystic rose?

Such ancient myths are long since belied.
What's human now is shared. That's right.
But still I swear I saw it flicker over you,
or was deceived by my own delight.

The Corner Table

Ansaphones presage the final text:
I have to take a step back.
And suddenly it's December, dim platforms,
late trains, half-finished teas left on dank stands.
The rhythm of the rails cannot numb
the pain that tightens in the chest,
as the heart feeds on its emptiness.

I gaze out on the ruined fields,
thinking of that small hotel down South,
its striped awning flapping in the breeze.
Long nights beneath the vine, late breakfasts on the quay,
cliff-walks scaring the larks up out of the grass —
none of this will now be ours,
as other guests book into our happiness.

Instead, wandering aimless in the evening streets,
I pass the bar where we used to meet
and glimpse through the rosy glass
two strangers sitting at our table,
gazing into each other's eyes.
It's that moment. The decision. Their time.
I wish them better words than mine.

The Harbour

This is the one I like best —
you, with your back to the camera
on the quayside in the blue-gray dress,
gazing out past the *molo* to the open sea.

It must have been that last evening in Ithaca,
amidst the silver olives and the orange scent,
watching the fishing-boats towards evening
ploughing out into the limpid blue…

How can it be I remember so vividly
the sunburnished capstan, the creak of the ropes,
the sighing of the rigging in the breeze,
even the cries of the children across the water?

It is a kind of nostalgia, yes,
but for something that never was, and yet,
stronger than the flat plane of memory
where the photograph replaces the event.

And though we were never there, nor wed, nor meant.
how that harbour scene stays in my head,
and leaves me wondering if a life is led
to discover what it should have been.

Sussex Blues

Spring blunders on without us,
lavishing itself on ditch and crown.
The first blue butterflies skitter out
across the greening down.

Not even hailstorms can halt them,
no matter how the stones may drum,
what is now revealed in blossom
cannot close or be undone.

How should we then stop what's opened
in our hearts, and to ourselves pretend?
No more could the chrysalis reseal
than you again call me your friend.

Eden II

Indian summer has baked the track.
One lone flower stars the hedge.
The gates are gone, the borders over,
and the trees, beyond their fruitfulness,
have lifted their branches out of reach.

The grizzled serpent feels my tread,
raises his head among the raspberry canes.
She is sitting over coffee on the step,
half-surprised I've come to pay my respects,
under the covenant of old friends.

Honeybees still hover among the pots.
It should be easier, with lives lived,
to talk of those once raw events,
but the silence deepens now
under the weight of the unsaid.

The hills develop in the morning mist.
A pair of wings swoops below the treeline.
So your work has brought you happiness?
Why yes. Yet still I can't admit it was her beauty
first made me want to impress.

A swallow slices the September air.
The truth is there, as if beneath a lifted stone.
You needed more than my nakedness then.
You were too young, too intense,
all I wanted was to dance and dress.

And now? One foot traces the regret.
The breeding heat is done.
The roused serpent lowers his head.
Come back, if you ever need to rest.
Age is the path to innocence.

6. Harvest Home

Canal Time

Down by the hump-backed bridge,
where the Grand Union
sets the pace of midsummer,
I watch my sons wind the windlass,
lean their backs into the beam
and swing the mitred lock-gates
to help the barges through.
Such work is leisure now,

but the bargee's boy has the accent still,
tells me he's turning fifteen,
the age I must have last fished here,
with my back to this red-brick mill.
It's inhabited now, *rustique*,
drying-holes glazed to lights.
sills planted with geraniums,
the wharf gone to grass and cycle path.

I lend my back to the beam.
A waft of weed, silt and fish.
The sense of something moving far below,
as if I were pushing at a gate
into a slower scape of time,
before these willows took their shape,
when the mill breathed out its malted breath
into the chugging, coal-smoked afternoon.

But it's not the past returning,
rather the present that extends —
the birds moving in their continuum,
the minnows rising, their perfect rings,
the bargee tinkering with his engine.
Call it *canal time*, the lower pulse
that beats, for example, in the tree,
a kind of witness, without memory.

And for the duration of that swing,
our feet overlap with all those
who pushed upon these iron steps,
with those who will follow yet
this custom by the water's edge,
as if a giant key were turned
to unlock the living moment
with the fellowship of the dead.

Gabriel

Firstborn
In Gabriel's eyes
the window comprehended
and what is beyond.

In the Mirror
At first he saw someone else
in a stranger's arms,
then recognized himself
in mine and laughed.

While I saw someone else,
rounder, holding him,
hardly recognized
the prodigal father.

Second Threshold
He crawls to the front door,
blinking in the sun,
prepares to cross
the second threshold
into the light.

Independent Play
When I open the door,
he's playing alone tonight.
I'm building a castle, he says.
He has begun without me
the long construction
of his own life.

Relay

I walk behind, considering
the same unpromising skies
my father walked under
the mornings I outran him.
He forges ahead,
twenty, now fifty yards,
before he turns at my call,
checks with half a smile,
ready at the corner
as if to receive the baton
to run the next leg
in a faster time.

Four Forty

No longer indulged,
he outdistances me.
I feel my heart complain,
leave me behind, son,
it's your race now, your line.

Penmarche

He is the lead bike
while the shadow of my head
nudges his back-wheel.

At The Barrier

Good luck!
He goes through.
I wait at the barrier,
watch him bounce down the platform,
press the button
and step aboard the train.

The doors slide shut,
but still I wait.
Until the whistle blows,
and the 9.02 pulls out on time,
London bound,
where I once made my way.

Now I know
he can go on without me.

Helen

Mine is the beauty
that rivals the brain,
wastes its desire,
random as rain.

Your glance is a javelin
flung from afar,
the weapon that wounds
leaving no scar.

Yet you go on looking
with onlooker's lust,
making me live
long after dust.

Poet, imagine
what burden I bore,
loved by so many,
hated by more.

What could you add
that would increase me,
buried in the shade
of the tamarisk tree?

Heap no more words
upon Helen's shrine,
pour her libations,
a cup of sweet wine.

Then you might see her,
fourteen and carefree,
your smiling daughter
fresh out of the sea.

Chichester Walls

How long did these walls hold firm?
There never was a century
when they were not breached
by cannon, storm, ivy and slump.
The burghers did their patchwork
but only if Messrs Corn and Mutton's duty
were reckoned in straight columns,
and the town chest grudgingly allowed.

What's now left is gapped
and stubby as a cobbler's bite.
The gates are long since gone
in all but name, proving too narrow
for the mail-coach and the wain;
and the bastions, built to withstand
whatever the enemy could sling,
reduced to shop and bogus inn.

High-minded youth, you'd think,
would never stand for this,
but lend its ardour to the wall's defence,
to preserve the city's steadfastness.
Yet money erodes, and its makers are quick
to widen loopholes, stuff arrowslits.
So sons of sons let the whole endeavour fall,
to bring the road and rail in,

Till only an idea of enclosure remains,
to be mulled over in summer,
as the stones turn evening pink,
vouchsafing us, in our beer, a glimpse
of the first citizens in their furs,
consulting timepieces, candlelit,
fiddling with their garnet rings,
waiting for the meeting to begin.

What excuse shall we give
when they examine what a poor fist
we have made upon our watch,
how feebly we managed to resist
when the siege-ladders clanged against the flints?
Conservation, gentlemen. We've done our bit.
While traffic runs through and over,
mindless of the charter and the cause.

Brighton Wall

This was once the old flint grid,
grey skeleton of the fishing port
still spooking in the backstreets,
marking time where the herring dried.

Patched with brick, bungaroosh and slap,
it grows accretions like a reef,
moss, cress, iron-stubs, plugs of gum,
sweet-wrappers stuffed into cracks.

Its ragged edges are capped like teeth
and filled with compromises of cement,
to smooth the post for the latest fence,
bodging the present to the past's intent.

We might delve its archive for events —
the parting tears, the urgent slash,
the rough-hewn shag on trembling legs,
the overnightings of a vanished tramp,

but this is *our* history, not *its* time —
where the hammer rings, the distance barks,
and the sun adds my shadow to the shadows
of the becalmed fishermen mending their nets.

The Sycamore Declines

Older than the corner,
it refuses to be confined
by paving, tarmac, wall,
offering uphill shade
beneath which, in heat,
the young or broken
are grateful to recline.

It has five seasons,
and in the fourth,
call it *the slow,*
the tree stands back,
serving notice on its tenants,
shrinking its leaves
to green-black rind.

Come Hallowe'en,
it moves in threads,
sifting the wind,
flinging its random keys.
Once more the head
lets in the sky,
entering its long decline.

Great teacher who never speaks,
who stands above
the morning and the evening tide,
show the quick and living
how to slow,
to sacrifice, winter
and be wise.

On Falmer Pond

The path from the station has disappeared,
lost now under the car parks for the stadium.
I endure ten minutes along the narrow verge
stumbling over lobbed cans and motor sludge
until, after a junction and a crossing,
I reach the stub of the old village road,
the relief of grass and trees around the pond.

The beasts that watered here are gone.
The carp rise in the late afternoon sun.
There is the sense of *afterwards*,
in which the ducks and Canada Geese
fuss and huff among the rushes.
An anxious couple flinch on a bench,
trying discreetly to end their open-air affair.

Who cares? Not the church. It's locked.
The notice-board announces the Risen Christ
beside a Smartwater warning to the thief.
I park myself on the graveyard's sunken seat,
(in memory of an Ethel from the Forties).
A busy churchbody arrives with the key,
but quickly shuts up again and drives on.

This is how the village ends, I guess,
becoming the picture postcard we kept
through war and boom and slump,
a place now for Sundays and the complaining aunts.
A willow weeps within the pond
in mourning for the world that's passed.
I tell the dead I shan't be long…

But then a rook caws…a tail-fin flips…aeons align —
the earth shakes, all around me the headstones flatten,
and the dead (including Ethel), layer on layer, arise,
spluttering and coughing, pushing back the tomb-lids,
tearing through the downland grass like moles,
sitting erect, shaking off their disbelief,
roaring their praises as the home team goes in front.

Harvest Home

Beneath the red-gold chesnut,
the priest is early, shifting from foot to foot.
It feels like Sunday with an empty church.
He's glad for once to see the councillor,
who's hoping to get away quickly in the car.
Not much interest, would you say, father?

But on the stroke of five
there is a sense of wheels juddering to a stop,
and, in twos and threes, they start to come
out of the shops and offices, up the hill,
leaving screens swimming, tills unchecked,
as if this were remembrance, a duty not yet derelict.

The estate agent shakes his head and closes up.
The postman has cut short his nap.
Telephonists, still wired, totter along in clogs
that once kept dairymaids out of the mud.
There are ribbons, favours, mascots, hats.
Someone's even brought a fox.

The woman from number 43 pitches up,
dragging her flatulent Labrador.
What's all this in aid of, father?
She's offering him a jar of ancient chutney
capped with fresh doiley and rubber band.
I didn't want to come empty-handed.

The Kapoors, not knowing quite what to expect
have turned out the children in their best.
Shefali unwinds a length of sari on request,
to show the fineness of the peacock silks.
Reggae starts from a beat-box somewhere,
and a bottle is already doing the rounds.

All-day drinkers from the pub
shape up defiantly for posterity,
pints held in place of rifles to their chests.

They ape the squeaky student with the mobile
relaying what's happening back to his flat.
It's wild. You've got to get here quick!

The councillor clears his throat, wondering
if, after all, someone should say a few words,
but thinks twice when the woman
who used to teach him at the school
is suddenly up on a chair, shouting instructions:
in a bit, Mrs Delaney…children down the front…

The young are everywhere at once,
the old reluctant to shift. It's slow,
but finally the rows arrange themselves,
and every face has found a gap in which to fit.
Towards me, now. Say…Cheese!
Again! Somebody moved!

Then out of nowhere — *One more for the Skylark…*
The breath is broken, the accent still intact,
he sports a woodcock feather in his hat,
crouching down in front with his collie
who strangely senses where the camera is —
I've never missed one yet.

There is a lull, the light comes right,
the tree seems to spread out its arms
and usher in the shy and half-willing,
a kind of sympathy branches out through the limbs,
and everyone knows as the shutter clicks —
this is the one they'll print.